THE ANCIENT EGYPTIAN

EGYPTIAN

FACTS *of* LIFE

Written by
JACQUELINE MORLEY

Illustrated by
MARK BERGIN & JOHN JAMES

Created & Designed by
DAVID SALARIYA

MACDONALD YOUNG BOOKS

Contents

INTRODUCTION

ANCIENT EGYPT, seen from our point of view, is very ancient indeed – about five thousand years old. At that far point in time the people of the Nile valley, in the north-east corner of Africa, became united under one ruler and the kingdom of Egypt was created. Its story is not only old, it is also extremely long. Egyptian civilization had existed for over two and a half thousand years when the ancient Greek historian Herodotus described it around 450 BC. It was even older when the Roman empire swallowed it in 30 BC.

Three thousand years is a great deal of history – time for many kings to reign, to build great monuments and to make Egypt rich and powerful; time for the pyramids to become ancient monuments to the ancient Egyptians themselves. Yet in all those centuries the beliefs and the way of life of the Egyptian people changed very little. They had great respect for the wisdom of their ancestors; their way was the right way, so what reason was there to change?

Many centuries later, scholars divided this long period of ancient Egyptian history into several periods. The most important are known as the Old Kingdom, from c2686 to 2181 BC, the Middle Kingdom from c1991 to 1786 BC and the New Kingdom from c1568 to 1085 BC.

FACT: IN ANCIENT EGYPT, FLOODS WERE GOOD NEWS

THE ANCIENT EGYPTIANS depended on the River Nile for life itself. The little rain that fell upon their desert land was not enough to make crops grow. Each year Egyptians were saved from starvation as if by a miracle. At about the time of year that we call October the level of the Nile rose and water poured over the parched land. After a few weeks the river shrank back to its usual size, leaving a layer of fertile black mud to enrich the soil. Today we know that the flood is caused by tropical rainstorms many thousands of kilometres to the south, near the Nile's source.

The ancient Egyptians did not know this. They believed that the flood was sent by the gods, as a sign they were pleased with the Egyptian nation.

When the flood came people thanked Hapi, the Nile god. Honouring the gods was very important to the Egyptians. (Foreigners noted what an extremely religious people they were.) They feared that if they did not express their gratitude the gods might not send the life-giving flood.

MEDITERRANEAN SEA

DELTA

STEP PYRAMID, SAQQARA

BENT PYRAMID, DASHUR

limestone quarry

MOST EGYPTIANS lived in the fertile strip along the Nile, the highway linking all parts of the kingdom. To control his long realm, the pharaoh, the king of Egypt, sent officials up and down the river, to ensure local affairs were managed properly and to report back to him.

RIVER NILE

ABYDOS

THEBES

RED SEA

granite quarry

PEASANTS built their villages on mounds above flood level, and moved their animals to higher ground as the Nile rose. When the land was flooded farmers went fishing, making boats by lashing together bundles of the papyrus reeds that grew by the river.

FARMERS planted crops when the flood went down. Bullocks pulled the wooden ploughs, men scattered seed and herded animals behind to trample it in.

Farming Facts:
The Egyptians divided the year into three seasons: flood time, seed time and harvest.

The commonest crops were wheat and barley, vegetables, figs, melons, pomegranates and vines.

Flood water was stored in a network of canals, to water the fields when the flood had gone. It was vital to stop the water seeping away, so a government department was in charge of keeping the canals in good repair.

REAPERS (left) cut the ripe corn with wooden sickles edged with sharp flints. Women and children came behind, to collect any fallen ears of corn.

CATTLE trampled over the cut corn (left) to remove the grain from the ears. Then the grain was tossed into the air (right), so the breeze blew the light, useless chaff away.

FARMERS had to pay part of their crop to the pharaoh, as tax. Officials inspected the fields and decided the amount to be paid. Scribes noted every payment.

GRAIN paid as tax was stored in the pharaoh's huge granaries. In times of famine it was used to feed the people, but normally it went to pay the pharaoh's officials.

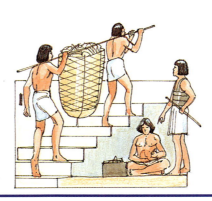

AS THE GRAIN was carried into the granaries (left), scribes kept detailed records of the amount each farmer had paid.

FACT: THE PHARAOH WAS A GOD ON EARTH

THE ANCIENT EGYPTIANS believed that their pharaoh was the god Horus, son of Re, the sun god. When a pharaoh died he was united with the sun and a new Horus ruled on earth. The prosperity of Egypt, its wonderful yearly flood, its superiority to all other nations (in Egyptian eyes) proved that this was so.

Being a god, there was nothing, in theory, which the pharaoh could not do. He was head of the government and high priest of every temple. In practice, officials did most of the work, in his name.

> **Pharaoh Facts:**
> The title Pharaoh ('Great House') described the king's majesty.
>
> When a pharaoh died, Re's divinity (and the kingship of Egypt) was passed on through the pharaoh's eldest daughter. Whoever claimed the throne married her to confirm his right to rule, even if he were her brother.
>
> A woman could be pharaoh, but this was most unusual. Queen Hatshepsut ruled c1478-1469 BC.

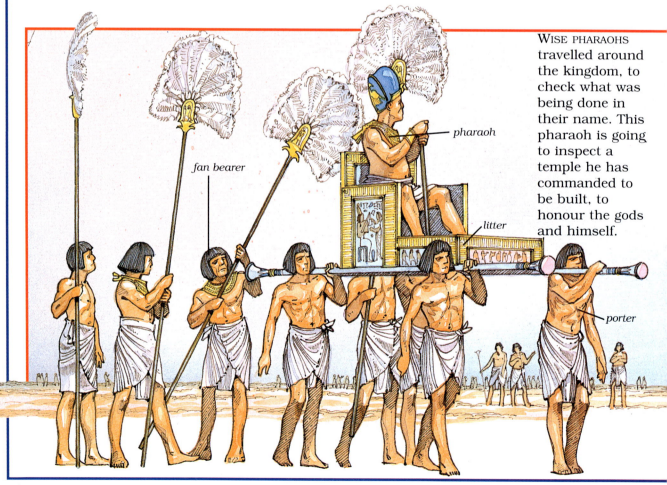

fan bearer

pharaoh

litter

porter

WISE PHARAOHS travelled around the kingdom, to check what was being done in their name. This pharaoh is going to inspect a temple he has commanded to be built, to honour the gods and himself.

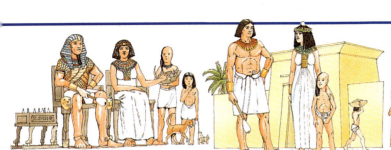

THE PHARAOH often had several wives, but only one was queen.

IF HE DIED while his children were young, the queen became regent.

EACH PROVINCE had a governor who lived there with his family.

HEADS of large ministries took care of central government.

HEADS of the army, the law, the treasury and irrigation.

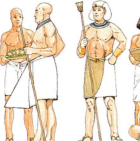

THE HEAD of building works surveying a site for a new temple.

THE CHIEF SCRIBE: his department stored the royal correspondence.

THE OVERSEER of granaries; the controller of the royal household.

THE CONTROLLER was in charge of an army of palace servants: cooks,

butlers, dressers, litter carriers, fan bearers and wardrobe keepers.

THE VIZIER, the pharaoh's chief minister, was the most important official. He kept an eye on the work of all the others and gave the pharaoh a daily report on their work. He also judged important legal cases. Left: he is sentencing thieves who have broken into a tomb and taken valuables belonging to the dead. This was a very serious crime.

FACT: IN EGYPT ALL CHILDREN WERE WELCOME

YOU WOULD have been safer born into an Egyptian family than in many others of ancient times. Foreigners were surprised to see that in Egypt no baby was ever left to die, no matter how poor its parents – which was not the case in many other lands.

If your father was rich – a member of the pharaoh's court, a high priest or an important official – you had a big house and a garden to play in, a country estate to visit and lots of servants. But there were far more poor families than rich ones, and for the poor life was very different. Most people were peasants, labourers or humble craftsmen and led hard lives. As soon as their children were old enough, they had to work too.

WOMEN used birthing stools like this to help them deliver their babies. They breast fed their children until they were about three years old.

WELL-OFF PARENTS sent their sons to school, and craftsmen's sons might go too, though they soon had to leave to join their father's trade. Girls were taught at home. School teachers were strict, and much time was spent copying out ancient texts and learning them by heart.

ROOFS gave precious extra space in the cramped town houses. Families worked and ate there under a shelter by day and slept there at night. Children played on the roofs, running from one to another.

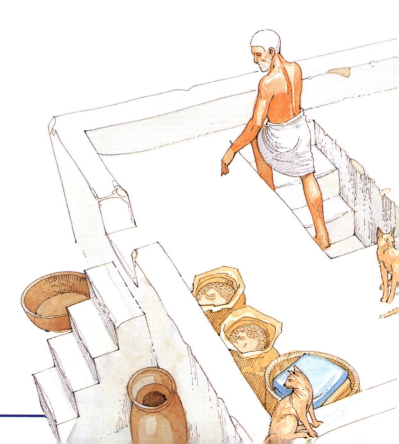

Family Facts:

Marriages were usually arranged. Many couples married when the bride was about 12 years old and the groom about 15.

Divorce was legal. A wife could challenge her divorce in court if she thought it unjust.

In many ways women were treated as men's equals. They could earn wages and own property. If they divorced, they could keep their children and property and marry again.

CHILDREN were expected to help their parents a lot, but they still had time for games. Leap-frog, ball games, tug of war and wrestling were popular. Indoors they played with dolls and wooden toys. Grown-ups played board-games with dice and counters. Dogs and cats were popular pets.

PEOPLE believed the ram-headed god Khnum made each child (and its 'ka' or spirit double) on a potter's wheel (below), then put it in the mother's body. Scarab amulets (left) were said to help couples have children.

TAWERET, a hippopotamus goddess, helped women give birth.

A MAN who ill-treated his wife could be taken to court by her angry relatives.

WHEN a child was born, its parents consulted a horoscope to learn its future, believing the stars influenced everyone's life.

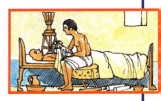

A MARRIED WOMAN makes her will. She could chose who would have her property when she died.

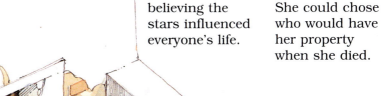

FACT: ALL HOMES WERE MADE OF MUD

IN ANCIENT EGYPT people built their houses of the material available – Nile mud. Mud was mixed with chopped straw and made into bricks which were baked hard in the sun. All dwellings, even the pharaoh's magnificent palace, were made of mud. Only temples and tombs were built of stone. On important buildings the bricks were covered with splendidly glittering, many-coloured tiles. Grand houses had pillared entrances and many rooms – a set of private rooms for the owner, another for the women and children of the family, rooms for servants, for washing and dressing, reception rooms and cool courtyards for entertaining guests. The poor lived crowded together in narrow streets.

CLAY MODELS of houses (like the one above with a farmyard in front) have been found in ancient Egyptian tombs.

Facts about Homes:
Rooms were brightly painted, sometimes with birds or flowers, or with the figures of protective gods.

Rich people had elegant chairs, tables and beds, often carved and gilded, or inlaid with precious woods, but most homes had only a few stools and small tables, and mats for sleeping on.

Cooking was often done out of doors, over a brazier or a fire made in a hole in the ground.

town wall

rooftop workshops

workers' houses

palmwood supports

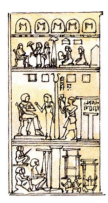

A MERCHANT'S HOUSE (left) from a wall painting in a New Kingdom tomb. There is a weaving workshop on the ground floor and living rooms above. Bins to store grain are on the roof.

THE SCENE below is based on the excavated remains of a Middle Kingdom walled town, created by a pharaoh for workers building his pyramid. Inside, the houses were like the craftsman's house (above right).

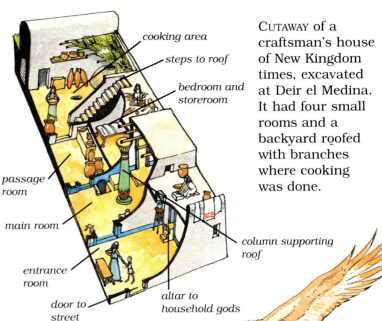

cooking area

steps to roof

bedroom and storeroom

passage room

main room

entrance room

door to street

altar to household gods

column supporting roof

Cutaway of a craftsman's house of New Kingdom times, excavated at Deir el Medina. It had four small rooms and a backyard roofed with branches where cooking was done.

temple

small windows to keep out the sun's glare

FACT: EGYPTIANS WENT SHOPPING WITHOUT MONEY

EXCEPT in rare famine years, no one starved in Egypt. The Nile's flood and constant sunshine produced such good crops that even peasants with tiny patches of land could grow enough wheat, vegetables and fruit to live on. Those who could afford meat ate pork, mutton, goat, goose, duck or wild game. Beef was a luxury because cows needed good land that was better used for crops. Hens were unknown until the New Kingdom (c1568–1085 BC), when some were imported from Syria.

There were no shops. Townsfolk bought what they needed from farmers and craftsmen who sold their wares from stalls in the streets. Money had not been invented, so shopping was done by bartering – exchanging goods of equal value. Wages and taxes were paid in the form of food, goods or services.

MAKING BEER. Barley bread was soaked in water sweetened with dates. The liquid fermented to make beer.

Food and Shopping Facts:

Bread was full of grit because bits of the grindstones got into the flour and sand was added to the grain to speed up the grinding. The sand and grit wore away people's teeth.

Fish and pork were 'unclean'. That meant they were not acceptable as offerings to the gods. People who were able to choose did not eat them.

Big purchases were sometimes agreed in writing to avoid arguments. A scribe sold an ox for a fine linen tunic and two everyday ones, beads for a necklace and several sacks (probably of grain, but this is not recorded).

BARTERING, from a wall painting. Each item had to be bargained for.

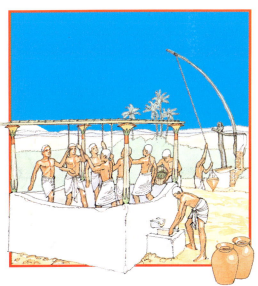

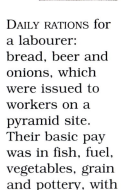

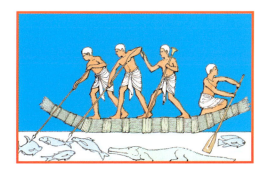

DAILY RATIONS for a labourer: bread, beer and onions, which were issued to workers on a pyramid site. Their basic pay was in fish, fuel, vegetables, grain and pottery, with beer and dates from time to time. At festivals they got bonuses.

THE NILE provided poor people with a cheap source of food. Its waters were full of fish and its marshes were home to huge flocks of birds – duck, crane and teal. If hunters caught too many to eat or sell, the surplus were gutted, dried in the sun and then stored in jars of salt.

THESE MEN are treading grapes in a big trough, to make wine. Most wine came from vineyards in the Nile delta.

YOU DID NOT take a purse to market, but it was no use going empty-handed. People brought things made at home – mats, cloth, cakes or bread – to exchange for farm produce and craftware – pottery, sandals, jewellery and toys.

FACT: FINE WHITE LINEN WAS ALWAYS IN FASHION

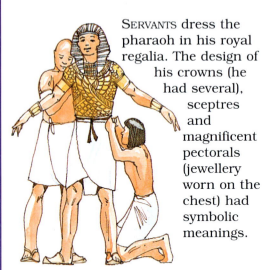

SERVANTS dress the pharaoh in his royal regalia. The design of his crowns (he had several), sceptres and magnificent pectorals (jewellery worn on the chest) had symbolic meanings.

NOTHING shows more clearly how deeply the ancient Egyptians respected tradition than their way of dressing. In 3000 years it hardly changed at all. (It didn't occur to the Egyptians to alter what was satisfactory already.) People wore tunics or loincloths of plain cotton or linen, usually white. Egypt was famous for the quality of its linen, which was exported far and wide. The best was gauzy-thin and very expensive. People displayed their wealth by the quality of the cloth they wore and the value of their jewellery.

Facts about Dressing:

Men and women lined their eyes with green and black make up. The colours came from ground-up minerals.

White clothes need frequent washing, and show the pride the Egyptians took in cleanliness. Wealthy homes had 'shower' rooms (where a servant tipped water over the bather) and quite ordinary ones had lavatories – a seat over a big bowl of sand.

To be pure enough to serve the gods, priests washed several times a day and shaved their heads and bodies.

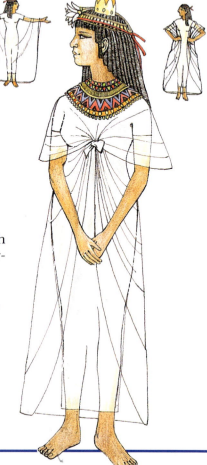

WORKERS wore simple loincloths. Some were made of soft leather, for hard wear.

MOST MEN wore a wrapped skirt. The front was often draped to form a panel.

A WOMAN'S basic garment was a narrow shift, often with shoulder straps. Rich women added a wide over-garment of transparent linen, drawn in and knotted under the breast. Sometimes the linen was pressed into countless tiny pleats.

Both men and women wore broad neck-ornaments and tightly ringleted wigs of human hair or wool.

NECKLACES, rings and earstuds (left). The ancient Egyptians liked bold jewellery. The rich wore gold inlaid with semiprecious stones, while poor people wore collars of beads.

TOILET ARTICLES: comb, razor and tweezers above, and a mirror of polished copper and two cosmetic holders below. There were many different cosmetics – for curing baldness, freckles, crow's feet; for tinting the eyebrows; for making a rival's hair fall out. A recipe survives for an oil 'to change an old man into a young one'.

ENTERTAINMENT at the court of the pharaoh (right). The women guests wear cones of scented wax upon their heads. As the wax melted it released its fragrance to refresh the wearer. Servants also bring them sweet-smelling lotus flowers (the woman on the opposite page has bound one on her wig). The lotus, a Nile water lily, was a sacred flower, the symbol of the sunrise.

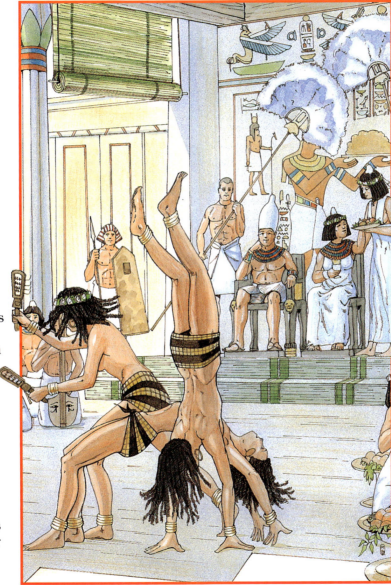

SANDALS (left). People usually went barefoot, but might take sandals to wear if needed.

THE PROFESSIONAL DANCERS above wear only a hip-band. People who did strenuous jobs often worked naked. Very young children went naked too. Putting on one's first clothes was a sign of leaving babyhood behind.

FACT: THE PYRAMIDS WERE ROYAL TOMBS

WHEN A PHARAOH DIED he was buried in a tomb designed to protect his body for ever. For if his body were destroyed, his ka, which returned to the body to receive offerings of food, would have nowhere to go and would die. Then the pharaoh could not be united with the sun, the gods would withdraw their blessings and disaster would follow.

Early royal tombs were covered by flat-topped mounds of mud-bricks. Later, the mounds had stepped sides. Finally stone pyramids were built.

TOOLS for quarrying, shaping and laying stone.

QUARRYING LIMESTONE. Quarrymen levelled the rock-face, then drove in wooden wedges to split it into blocks. Stone was dragged to the river and taken by boat to the pyramid site.

Pyramid Facts:

The Step Pyramid, built c2646 BC for the pharaoh Zoser, was the first building in the world to be made entirely of specially shaped stones. The first pyramids with smooth sides were built around 2600 BC. When new, a pyramid gleamed white in the sun. Some had gilded capstones – the stone forming the tip.

Most of a pyramid was solid. From its entrance a narrow passage led to the burial chamber deep within.

Each pharaoh was buried with fabulous treasures – all the weapons, jewellery, sacred objects, clothes and furniture he would need in the next world. To confuse tomb-robbers, the entrance was disguised to look like the rest of the pyramid's outer surface.

Pyramid-building continued for nearly a thousand years. Later ones were made of brick or rubble with just a facing of stone, and have mostly crumbled away.

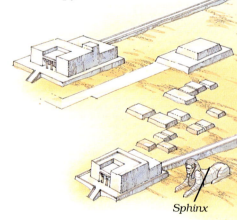

Sphinx

THE PYRAMIDS OF GIZA, built c2566–2500 BC. They were surrounded by temples, smaller pyramids and tombs, and guarded by a huge stone sphinx, still there today.

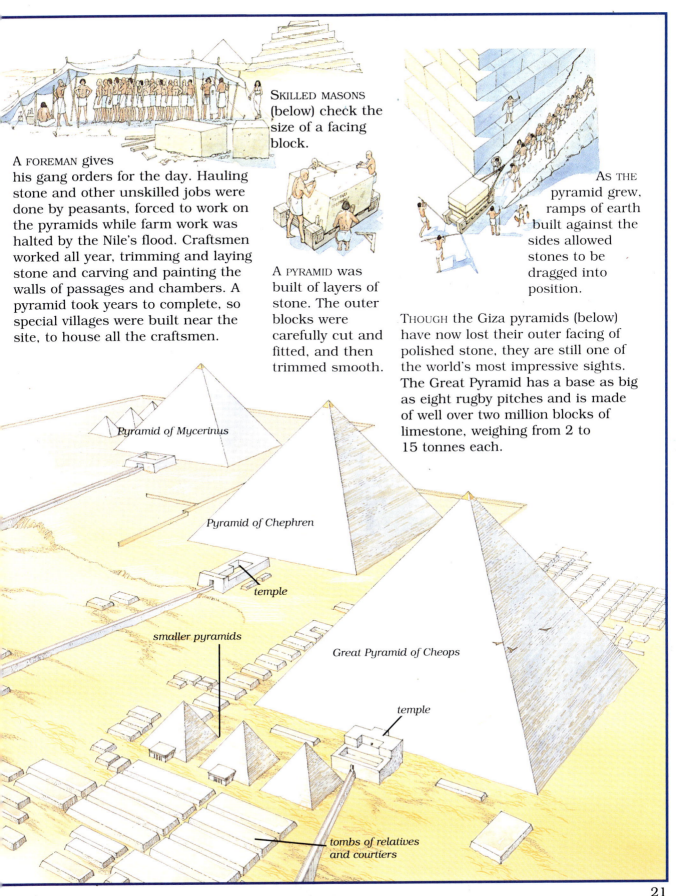

SKILLED MASONS (below) check the size of a facing block.

A FOREMAN gives his gang orders for the day. Hauling stone and other unskilled jobs were done by peasants, forced to work on the pyramids while farm work was halted by the Nile's flood. Craftsmen worked all year, trimming and laying stone and carving and painting the walls of passages and chambers. A pyramid took years to complete, so special villages were built near the site, to house all the craftsmen.

A PYRAMID was built of layers of stone. The outer blocks were carefully cut and fitted, and then trimmed smooth.

AS THE pyramid grew, ramps of earth built against the sides allowed stones to be dragged into position.

THOUGH the Giza pyramids (below) have now lost their outer facing of polished stone, they are still one of the world's most impressive sights. The Great Pyramid has a base as big as eight rugby pitches and is made of well over two million blocks of limestone, weighing from 2 to 15 tonnes each.

Pyramid of Mycerinus

Pyramid of Chephren

temple

smaller pyramids

Great Pyramid of Cheops

temple

tombs of relatives and courtiers

FACT: TEMPLES WERE THE HOUSES OF THE GODS

LONG AGO, so the ancient Egyptians believed, the gods had lived on earth and shown men how to live good lives. Later they departed to the Land of the Dead (a happy place), but the ka of each god still had an earthly house – a temple dedicated to it. Every town and village had at least one temple to a local god. The god lived in the innermost part of the temple, where its image was kept in a shrine. Priests waited on the god daily, washing and dressing the image and offering it incense and food. All these actions were done in the name of the pharaoh, for only he was worthy to serve the gods.

Many temples owned large estates, with farms and workshops. Temples were also centres of learning, with schools, libraries and teaching hospitals.

TEMPLES, like tombs, were eternal dwellings, so they were built of stone, and decorated with painting, carving and gilding.

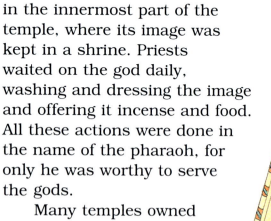

pylon (entrance gate)

obelisk

TEMPLE SCHOOLS trained boys to become scribes – professional record keepers. Scribes were needed to keep accounts and write reports. They could rise to high office.

forecourt

Hathor   Horus   Isis   Maat   Atum   Khons   Geb   Harakhty   Osiris

ALL TEMPLES had the same plan: a pylon or gateway, a pillared court, and a series of halls leading to the sanctuary.

sanctuary

pillared hall

side chamber

pillared courtyard

THE ANCIENT Egyptians had many gods. Above are some that were honoured throughout Egypt. Other, lesser, gods just had local fame. Long before the time of the pharaohs, Egypt had been a land of separate chiefdoms, each with its own gods which local people still remembered.

Facts about the Gods:

Only the pharaohs and priests could enter the main temple building and approach its god. Other people left their offerings in the courtyard.

The best loved god was Osiris. The myth of his death and return to life as king of the underworld gave people hope of life after death.

Bes, a smiling dwarf-god, protected homes from evil spirits.

TEMPLE and tomb inscriptions were written in hieroglyphs, signs representing words or sounds. Scribes wrote a quick, simplified form of them on paper made from papyrus reeds.

FACT: CRAFTSMEN WORKED TO GLORIFY THE GODS

EVERY TOWN AND VILLAGE had its craftsmen – potters, weavers, carpenters, metalworkers – who supplied people's everyday needs. But there were other needs that were just as important. In the cities and on the temple estates highly skilled craftsmen, trained to work according to long-established sacred traditions, produced objects that were needed in the service of the gods: inlaid and gilded shrines, statues, vases and magnificent jewellery. These adorned the palaces, temples and royal tombs.

By Middle Kingdom times (c1991–1786 BC) many ordinary people also hoped for places in the Land of the Dead, and commissioned craftsmen to build them fine tombs.

A BUNDLE of artist's brushes made of reeds, and a holder for cakes of paint.

CUTTING PAPYRUS (above) to make paper from the reeds' pith. Paper was invented in Egypt.

PAINTERS decorate a temple (below), working from the top down, since the lower part is buried in earth.

THE EARTH, piled up as a ramp during building, is removed as the painting continues.

TOMB walls were painted. The design was marked with a grid for transfer to the wall.

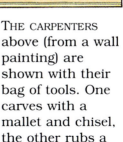

CARPENTERS (above) begin work on a shrine. One trims wood with an adze; another uses a bow-drill; a third saws planks after lashing the timber to a post to keep it steady.

THE CARPENTERS above (from a wall painting) are shown with their bag of tools. One carves with a mallet and chisel, the other rubs a surface smooth.

DRILLING out a vase shaped from stone. The Egyptians excelled at this difficult craft.

METALWORKERS made weapons, tools and jars by hammering or melting copper and bronze.

A POTTER turns the wheel with one hand and shapes the pot with the other.

COPPER SMELTING. Bellows helped raise the heat of the furnace. The liquid copper was set in moulds.

MODEL of a linen weaver's workshop. The ancient Egyptians wove on a horizontal loom, pegged into the ground. Though thread was spun by women in their spare time, weaving was usually a full-time craft, also often done by women. The woman on the right is winding thread.

Craft Facts:

Ptah, the local god of Memphis (the first capital of Egypt) was the god of craftsmen. The city was famous as a centre for all types of crafts.

Paper-making was the foundation of the pharaohs' government. Paper enabled people for the first time to write rapidly, with pen and ink, so creating an 'information super-highway' which made possible the highly organized Egyptian state.

African gold, ebony, amethysts, ivory and ostrich feathers were imported for Egyptian craftsmen.

GOLDSMITHS also worked with molten metal, or beat sheets of gold into the right shapes.

FACT: AN EVERLASTING BODY GAVE EVERLASTING LIFE

THE LAND OF THE DEAD, the Egyptians believed, was very like this world, but free from worries. For the spirit to live there, it needed an immortal body, so it was essential that a person's corpse should not decay. Corpses will not rot if they become completely dry, as happened when bodies were buried in the hot sand. This was the earliest form of Egyptian burial and poor people continued to be buried in this way. But in a tomb a body soon decayed. To avoid this it was made into what is termed a mummy.

A JACKAL-HEADED jar held the stomach, a human one the liver, a falcon the intestines and a baboon the lungs.

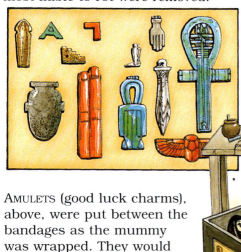

THE CORPSE was put on a stone embalming table with a drainage hole. There it was cut open and the internal organs that were most liable to rot were removed.

THE BODY was then packed round with natron (a type of salt) and left for up to 100 days, until quite dry.

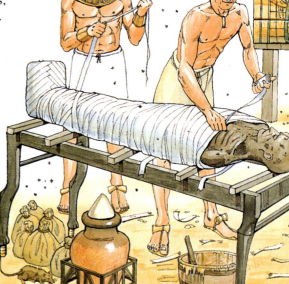

AMULETS (good luck charms), above, were put between the bandages as the mummy was wrapped. They would protect the dead person during the journey to the next world.

1   2   3   4

1 MUMMY of Pharaoh Seti I, c1304 BC.
2 Seti I's outer shroud.
3 Rich woman's inner coffin.
4 A pharaoh's gilded coffin case.

ONCE IT WAS DRY, the body was tightly wrapped in up to 20 layers of linen bandage, each layer waterproofed with resin. This took about 15 days and needed hundreds of metres of linen. To ensure that the dead person's ka would recognize its owner, a painted portrait mask of plaster was placed over the mummy's head. Pharaohs' masks were made of gold. Then the mummy was ready for its painted coffin. In New Kingdom times (c1568–1085 BC) these, too, were mummy-shaped and had one or more outer cases.

MODELS of objects (below) used in the Opening of the Mouth Ritual.

THE OPENING OF THE MOUTH ritual was held at the tomb. The mummy was touched with special objects, to enable it to see, hear and eat.

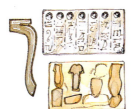

IN THE NEXT WORLD, Anubis, god of the dead, judged each heart. If its sins weighed more than the feather of truth it was devoured by a monster.

FACT: EGYPTOLOGISTS' DREAMS CAME TRUE – IN 1922

MOST OF OUR KNOWLEDGE of the ancient Egyptians comes from their tombs. (Their houses would also have taught us much, but most are buried under modern cities.) Royal tombs should have yielded many precious objects, but for many years Egyptologists could only find ones that had been robbed. Then, in 1922, they found a tomb barely touched since it was sealed over 3000 years earlier.

THE PHARAOH'S mummy was covered by this funeral mask of solid gold, weighing 10.2kg.

TUTANKHAMUN'S tomb at the moment of its discovery (below). Its contents are now in the Cairo Museum.

annexe

AMONG the jewels buried with Tutankhamun was this splendid gold and silver pectoral, inlaid with semi-precious stones, and bearing symbols of the sun and the moon.

antechamber

The tomb belonged to Tutankhamun, a New Kingdom pharaoh. In his own time he was not an important ruler, but now he is famous as the owner of the most magnificent ancient Egyptian treasures ever discovered. His tomb was discovered in 1922 by the British Egyptologist Howard Carter, in the Valley of the Kings, a royal burial place on the west bank of the Nile, opposite Thebes.

THE FIRST ROOM (the antechamber) was packed with objects piled haphazardly: chairs, stools, chests, vases, three gilded beds shaped like animals, boxes stuffed with clothes and food, weapons and the jumbled parts of two golden chariots. It seems that robbers were surprised by guards who thrust things back in disorder before resealing the tomb.

THE BURIAL CHAMBER was almost filled by a huge gilded shrine. There was another inside it, enclosing a third, and in that was a fourth, of solid gold. This held a yellow quartzite sarcophagus enclosing the mummy which lay in three separate mummy-shaped coffins. The treasury, guarded by a crouching jackal figure, held a shrine and many other precious objects.

Tutankhamun Facts:

Tutankhamun ruled from c1339–1329 BC. He was about 17 when he died. An X-ray of his skull revealed a thinning of the bone behind one ear, suggesting that he may have died from a head injury.

Tutankhamun, like other pharaohs of the time, was buried in a tomb cut into a rocky hillside. Pharaohs were no longer buried in pyramids because they were such obvious targets for robbers.

Tutankhamun's burial goods were magnificent, but his tomb was unfinished. Only the burial chamber had been levelled and decorated, suggesting hurried burial arrangements after an unexpected death.

burial chamber

treasury

ARMBAND of gold and lapis lazuli with a scarab, symbol of the sun.

MODEL of the type of boat used for travelling on the Nile.

BEYOND the antechamber was a smaller room, which Carter called the annexe, even more crammed with furniture.

CARTER uncovered steps cut into the rock. He inspects the sealed door (left) at the bottom, together with his patron, Lord Carnarvon.

ELEVEN model boats were in the tomb. After his death, the Egyptians' believed the pharaoh travelled the sky in the sun's boat.

LOSSARY

Adze Tool to trim wood, with the blade at right angles to the handle.

Bellows Leather bags, squeezed to produce a strong blast of air.

Bow-drill Drill encircled by the string of a small bow. As the bow was pushed backwards and forwards the string turned the drill.

Chaff Light, papery covering of grains of corn, separated from the grain during threshing.

Delta Flat, fan-shaped area of land formed by a river which has split into many small streams as it nears the sea.

Egyptologist Archaeologist or scholar who studies ancient Egypt.

Embalmer Someone who preserves dead bodies.

Fermenting Another method of making alcohol, this time using natural sugars and yeasts to work on a particular ingredient.

Irrigation Watering land artificially.

Lapis lazuli Blue semiprecious stone.

Litter Seat set on long poles and carried on the shoulders of porters.

Natron A natural salt, found in Egypt in a dry lake-bed in the western delta.

Patron Someone who provides money or support to help someone else.

Pectoral Ornament worn on the chest.

Pylon Ancient Egyptian entrance gate.

Quartzite Very hard rock, formed mostly of the common mineral, quartz.

Reaping Cutting and harvesting corn.

Regalia Emblems of royalty worn by a king or queen.

Sarcophagus Stone coffin.

Scarab Type of beetle.

Scribe Compiler of written records. The modern equivalent would range from an office clerk to a top civil servant.

Shrine Container with doors in which the image of a god is kept.

Shroud Cloth in which a body is wrapped for burial.

Smelt Obtain metal by melting the ore at a very high temperature.

Sphinx Statue with the body of a crouching lion, and the head of a ram, falcon or pharaoh.